To Mic...

With

G000144257

2.8·11·98

A Book of Prayers
for the First Years
of Marriage

This edition copyright © 1995 Lion Publishing
Illustrations copyright © 1995 Susan Pontefract

Published by
Lion Publishing plc
Sandy Lane West, Oxford, England
ISBN 0 7459 3359 9
Albatross Books Pty Ltd
PO Box 320, Sutherland, NSW 2232, Australia
ISBN 0 7324 1321 4

First edition 1995
10 9 8 7 6 5 4 3 2 1 0

Acknowledgments
The introduction is taken, in part, from *Discovering Prayer*,
copyright © 1985 Andrew Knowles.

Every attempt has been made to trace copyright holders of prayers.
If there have been any inadvertent omissions in the acknowledgments
we apologize to those concerned. Thanks go to:
The Central Board of Finance of the Church of England for material
from the ASB 1980, Church House Publications for material from
Services of Prayer and Dedication after a Civil Marriage; HarperCollins
Publishers Ltd for William Barclay from *The Plain Man's Book of Prayers*,
Christopher Idle; The Methodist Publishing House for material from
the Methodist Conference © 1975, Mothers Union Service and Prayer
Books, Union of Liberal and Progressive Synangogues.

A catalogue record for this book is available
from the British Library

Printed and bound in Singapore

A BOOK OF
PRAYERS
for the
FIRST YEARS
OF MARRIAGE

LION
Giftlines

Contents

Introduction

For some people, prayer seems to be the easiest thing in the world. Their prayer is thoughtful and fluent – and it seems they can turn it on and off like a tap!

But for most of us prayer is often quite hard and sometimes impossible. We can't help wondering whether God is really interested in the everyday things of our lives.

All of us who pray have times when we feel distant from God. There are occasions – perhaps even long periods of time – when we seem to be waiting for God. All we can say of him is that he doesn't seem to be around.

But as we continue to be available to him, we become aware that he is in fact all around us – and within us. He is everywhere and very close. As we open our hearts to God, he'll make himself known to us in his own way and in his own time. The particular way he deals with each of us can never be predicted, demanded or explained. It will be unique.

The unique nature of our relationship with God means that personal, spontaneous prayer is important. We 'talk' to God in prayer. But this is not always easy, especially if we are new to prayer. This is where written prayers can help. We have much in common as human beings, so other people's prayers can reflect the desires and fears of our own heart.

This anthology of prayers has been compiled for couples to use together in their first years of marriage. It is hoped that this collection will help couples to draw closer to God and to explore together a relationship with him. God, the creator of love and the designer of marriage, longs for us to seek him.

'God loves us. His motive in making us was love. His greatest longing is that we should get to know him, come to love him, enjoy his company. And when we talk to God or listen to him, head to head, heart to heart, this is prayer.'

Being with God

'When you have a great friend you may plan to spend a time with him and may be careful not to miss it. The use of the time is unlikely to be planned, but within the time news may be shared, requests may be made, regrets or gratitude may be spoken, and minds be exchanged, sometimes by talking and listening, and sometimes with little words or gestures . . .

To be with God wondering, that is adoration. To be with God gratefully, that is thanksgiving. To be with God ashamed, that is contrition. To be with God with others on the heart, that is intercession. The secret is the quest of God's presence: ''Thy face, lord, will I seek.'' '

MICHAEL RAMSEY

The Lord's Prayer

When Jesus was asked by his followers to
teach them to pray, he responded with a
model prayer – beautiful, balanced and brief.
It has come to be known as the Lord's Prayer.

Our Father in heaven,
hallowed be your name,
your kingdom come,
your will be done
on earth as it is in heaven.
Give us today our daily bread.
Forgive us our debts,
as we have forgiven our debtors.
And lead us not into temptation,
but deliver us from the evil one.

Our Love

Praise God
who has created courtship and marriage,
joy and gladness,
feasting and laughter,
pleasure and delight,
love, brotherhood, peace and fellowship.
THE METHODIST SERVICE BOOK

Father, we know that thou art the author of love; that the love which we bear each other is thy gift to us, precious in thy sight, precious in ours. Help us in the years ahead never lightly to regard that gift. We know that the relationship into which we are about to enter is more than moonlight and roses, much more than the singing of love songs and the whispering of our vows of undying affection. We know that in thy sight our marriage will be an eternal union. It is the clasping of our hands, the blending of our lives, the union of our hearts, that we may walk together up the hill of life to meet the dawn, together to bear life's burdens, to discharge its duties, to share its joys and sorrows. We know that our marriage will stand and endure — not by the wedding ceremony or by any marriage licence, but rather by the strength of the love which thou hast given us and by the endurance of our faith in each other and in thee, our Lord, the master of our lives.

And now, as alone with thee we plight this troth: we do promise thee, by thy help, to be faithful and true to each other and to thee who, having given us love and faith in thee, hast given us all things.

We thank thee that thy blessing will go down the years with us as a light on our way, as a benediction to the home we are about to establish. May that home always be a haven of strength and love to all who enter it — our neighbours and our friends. We thank thee. Amen.

PETER MARSHALL

The Lord God said, 'It is not good for the man to be alone.'

FROM THE BOOK OF GENESIS

Lord Jesus Christ, who by your presence and power brought joy to the wedding at Cana: bless those engaged to be married, that there may be truth at the beginning of their lives together, unselfishness all the way, and perseverance to the end. May their hopes be realised and their love for each other deepen and grow, that through them your name may be glorified.

MOTHERS' UNION SERVICE BOOK

That I may come near to her,
draw me nearer to you than to her;
that I may know her,
make me to know you more than her;
that I may love her with the perfect love
of a perfectly whole heart,
cause me to love you more than her
and most of all.
Amen.

That nothing may be between me and her,
be between us, every moment.
That we may be constantly together,
draw us into separate loneliness with
    yourself.
And when we meet breast to breast,
my God, let it be your own.
Amen. Amen.

TEMPLE GAIRDNER (1873–1928) BEFORE HIS MARRIAGE

Heavenly Father, send down upon us the dew of your heavenly grace in our married life, that we may have that joy in each other that passes not away; and having lived together in love here, may we ever live together in your glorious kingdom hereafter.

GEORGE HICKS (1642–1715)

Our Wedding Day

Shout for joy to the Lord, all the earth.
Worship the Lord with gladness; come
before him with joyful songs. Know that
the Lord is God. It is he who made us, and
we are his . . .

FROM PSALM 100

We thank you for the dawning of this day
and for your love renewed and shown every
morning. We pray for those who are to be
married today and ask that you will give
them great joy in the anticipation of the
fulfilment of their love. For their parents
we ask your nearness; for them a great
consciousness of belonging to each other;
and for all who are called to marriage a
faithfulness to their promises, through
Jesus Christ our Lord.

KENNETH THORNTON

O God of love, to thee we bow,
And pray for these before thee now,
That, closely knit in holy vow,
They may in thee be one.

When days are filled with pure delight,
When paths are plain and skies are bright,
Walking by faith and not by sight,
May they in thee be one.

When stormy winds fulfil thy will,
And all their good seems turned to ill,
Then, trusting thee completely, still
May they in thee be one.

Whate'er in life shall be their share
Of quickening joy or burdening care,
In power to do and grace to bear,
May they in thee be one.

WILLIAM VAUGHAN JENKINS (1868–1920)

Praise God, King of the universe, who has created all things, and man in his own image. Praise God, who has created courtship and marriage, joy and gladness, feasting and laughter, pleasure and delight, love, brotherhood, peace and fellowship.

Praise God, who has sent Jesus Christ to save us from sin and redeem our love from selfishness, and has given us the Holy Spirit to make us one with each other and with him.

METHODIST SERVICE BOOK

O God, by your mighty power you have made all things out of nothing, and having set in order the elements of the universe and made man to your image, appointed woman to be his inseparable helpmate, so that the woman's body took its origin in the flesh of man, thereby teaching that what you have been pleased to institute from one principle might never lawfully be separated.

O God, you have hallowed marriage by a mystery so excellent that in the marriage bond you prefigured the union of Christ with the Church.

O God, by whom woman is joined to man, and that union which you ordered from the beginning is endowed with a blessing which was not taken away, either by punishment for original sin or by the sentence of the flood . . .

May they both see their children's children to the third and fourth generation, and reach that old age which they desire. Through Jesus Christ our Lord.

GREGORIAN SACRAMENTARY (AD 590)

Holy God, who made mankind out of chaos and from his rib provided woman and yoked her as a help to him, because it pleased your great goodness that he should not be the only man on the earth; even now, Lord, stretch forth your hand from your holy dwelling-place, and fit together this your servant and this handmaid, that the woman may be fitted by you to the man. Yoke them together in unity of mind; crown them in love; unite them to be one flesh; graciously bestow on them the fruit of the womb, the enjoyment of children.

THE BYZANTINE RITE (EIGHTH CENTURY)

O God, our Father, whose greatest gift is love, bless —— and —— who today within thy presence will take each other in marriage. We thank thee that they have found such love and faith and trust in each other that they wish to take each other to have and to hold all the days of their life. Let nothing ever come between them, but throughout all the chances and the changes of life keep them for ever loving and for ever true. Keep them safe from illness, from poverty, from all trouble that would hurt them in any way. But, if any trial does come to them, grant that it may only drive them closer together and closer to thee. Grant unto them through all their days the perfect love which many waters cannot quench and which is stronger than even death itself: through Jesus Christ our Lord. Amen.

WILLIAM BARCLAY

O Father all creating
Whose wisdom, love, and power
First bound two lives together
In Eden's primal hour,
Today, to these thy children
Thine earliest gifts renew:
A home by thee made happy,
A love by thee kept true.

O Saviour, guest most bounteous
Of old in Galilee,
Vouchsafe today thy presence
With these who call on thee;
Their store of earthly gladness
Transform to heavenly wine,
And teach them, in the tasting,
To know the gift is thine.

O Spirit of the Father,
Breathe on them from above,
So mighty in thy pureness,
So tender in thy love;
That guarded by thy presence,
From sin and strife kept free,
Their lives may own thy guidance,
Their hearts be ruled by thee.

Except thou build it, Father,
The house is built in vain,
Except thou, Saviour, bless it,
The joy will turn to pain;
But nought can break the marriage
Of hearts in thee made one,
And love thy Spirit hallows
Is endless love begun.

JOHN ELLERTON (1826–93)

*May the Lord bless you, who granted Eve
for first-man Adam as a help like himself
lest he should live alone on the earth, and
ordered them to multiply, to bless, to grow,
and increase. Amen.*

*And may he who has deigned to join
these young people in their youthful age
send on them the fear and the love of his
holy name, and bring to life in them sons
and daughters born from them so that they
may grow in offspring and see their
children's children to the third and fourth
generation. Amen.*

*That rejoicing together they may be
able to pass through this present age, so
that they may be worthy of enjoying the
heavenly kingdom with the choirs of
angels. Amen.*

THE PONTIFICAL OF RODA (ELEVENTH CENTURY)

*O God, you have created man and woman
and have ordained them for the married
estate, have blessed them also with fruits of
the womb, and have typified therein the
sacramental union of your dear Son, the
Lord Jesus Christ, and the church, his
bride: we beseech your groundless goodness
and mercy that you would not permit this
your creation, ordinance and blessing to be
disturbed or destroyed, but graciously
preserve the same; through Jesus Christ our
Lord. Amen.*

MARTIN LUTHER (1483–1546)

We praise you, Father, that you have made all things, and hold all things in being. In the beginning you created the universe, and made mankind in your own likeness: because it was not good for them to be alone, you created them male and female; and in marriage you join man and woman as one flesh, teaching us that what you have united may never be divided.

We praise you that you have made this holy mystery a symbol of the marriage of Christ with his church, and an image of your eternal covenant with your people. And we pray for your blessing on this man and this woman, who come before you as partners and heirs together of your promises. Grant that this man may love his wife as Christ loves his bride the church, giving himself for it and cherishing it as his own flesh; and grant that this woman may love her husband and follow the example of those holy women whose praises are sung in the Scriptures. Strengthen them in your grace that they may be witnesses of Christ to others; let them live to see their children's children, and bring them at last to fullness of life with your saints in the kingdom of heaven; through Jesus Christ our Lord.

ALTERNATIVE SERVICE BOOK

Almighty God, giver of life and love,
bless ——— and ———. Grant them
wisdom and devotion in the ordering of
their common life, that each may be to the
other a strength in need, a counsellor in
perplexity, a comfort in sorrow, and a
companion in joy. And so knit their wills
together in your will, and their spirits in
your Spirit, that they may live together in
love and peace all the days of their life;
through Jesus Christ our Lord.

EPISCOPAL CHURCH, USA

*O perfect Love, all human thought
    transcending,*
Lowly we kneel in prayer before thy throne,
*That theirs may be the love which knows no
    ending,*
Whom thou for evermore dost join in one.

O perfect Life, be thou their full assurance
Of tender charity and steadfast faith,
*Of patient hope, and quiet brave
    endurance,*
*With childlike trust that fears nor pain
    nor death.*

*Grant them the joy which brightens earthly
    sorrow,*
*Grant them the peace which calms all
    earthly strife;*
*And to life's day the glorious unknown
    morrow*
That dawns upon eternal love and life.

DOROTHY FRANCES GURNEY (1858–1932)

We want to make our marriage work. But perhaps we shall need some help in order to live happily ever after. So if marriage really is a gift from you, God, please show us the right paths to take, and come with us on our journey.

MARION STROUD

*Thank you for your sweet and mysterious
gift of love — for all that we find in each
other that attracts and enriches. Make our
relationship begun in your presence —
gladdened by family and friends gathered
this day within the church — strong, holy,
and deathless. Bless the home that we plan
to build and keep together. Let its door be
ever open to things true and beautiful and
joyous. Let us so love and trust you in the
light that if dark skies are ever above us, we
shall know how near you are, how loving,
and how dependable.*

RITA SNOWDEN

Our Relationship
With God

*Come near to God and he will come
near to you.*

FROM THE BOOK OF JAMES

*We pray . . . that you may live a life
worthy of the Lord and may please him in
every way: bearing fruit in every good
work, growing in the knowledge of God,
being strengthened with all power
according to his glorious might so that you
may have great endurance and patience,
and joyfully giving thanks to the Father,
who has qualified you to share in the
inheritance of the saints in the kingdom of
light.*

FROM THE BOOK OF COLOSSIANS

Set our hearts on fire with love to you, O Christ our God, that in its flame we may love you with all our heart, with all our mind, with all our soul and with all our strength and our neighbours as ourselves, so that, keeping your commandments, we may glorify you, the giver of all good gifts.

EASTERN ORTHODOX CHURCH

O Lord, fill us, we beseech thee, with adoring gratitude to thee for all thou art for us, to us, and in us; fill us with love, joy, peace, and all the fruits of the Spirit. Amen.

CHRISTINA ROSSETTI (1830–95)

O God our heavenly Father, renew in us the sense of your gracious presence, and let it be a constant impulse within us to peace, trustfulness, and courage on our pilgrimage. Let us hold you fast with a loving and adoring heart, and let our affections be fixed on you, that so the unbroken communion of our hearts with you may accompany us whatever we do, through life and in death. Teach us to pray heartily, to listen for your voice within, and never to stifle its warnings. Behold, we bring our poor hearts as a sacrifice to you: come and fill your sanctuary, and suffer nothing impure to enter there. Let your divine Spirit flow like a river through our whole souls, and lead us in the right way till we pass by a peaceful death into the land of promise. Amen.

GERHARD TERSTEEGEN (1697–1769)

Almighty and everlasting God, grant that our wills be ever meekly subject to your will, and our hearts be ever honestly ready to serve thee. Amen.

ROMAN BREVIARY

O Lord, you know what is best for us, let this or that be done, as you shall please. Give what you will, and how much you will, and when you will. Deal with us as you think good, and as best pleases you. Set us where you will, and deal with us in all things just as you will. Behold, we are your servants, prepared for all things; for we desire not to live to ourselves, but unto you. And oh, that we could do it worthily and perfectly! Amen.

THOMAS À KEMPIS (1379–1471)

Our Relationship With Each Other

Submit to one another out of reverence for Christ.

FROM THE BOOK OF EPHESIANS

O God of peace, unite our hearts by your bond of peace, that we may live with one another continually in gentleness and humility, in peace and unity. O God of patience, give us patience in the time of trial, and steadfastness to endure to the end . . . Amen.

BERHARD ALBRECHT (1569–1636)

We thank you, God our Father,
for the joys of Christian marriage:
for the physical pleasure of bodily union,
the rich experience of mutual
*   companionship and family life,*
and the spiritual ecstasy of knowing and
*   serving Christ together.*
Help us to respond to your goodness
by recognizing you as the head of our
*   home,*
submitting to one another out of reverence
*   or Christ,*
bringing up our children in faith and
*   godly fear,*
and offering hospitality to the homeless.
We ask this in the name of Jesus our Lord.

MICHAEL BOTTING

O for love to be as gracious to another as one is to one's self, to put the same favourable interpretation upon their acts; to make the same liberal allowance for opinions; to choose among the many more generous motives . . . to be as jealous of today as one is wistful about yesterday!

ROBERT W. BARBOUR

Give us a sense of humour, Lord, and also things to laugh about. Give us the grace to take a joke against ourselves, and to see the funny side of the things we do. Save us from annoyance, bad temper, resentfulness against our friends. Help us to laugh even in the face of trouble. Fill our minds with the love of Jesus; for his name's sake.

A.G. BULLIVANT

O God, perfect us in love, that we may conquer all selfishness . . . Fill our hearts with your joy, and shed abroad in them your peace which passes understanding; that so those murmurings and disputings to which we are too prone may be overcome. Make us long-suffering and gentle, and thus subdue our hastiness and angry tempers, and grant that we may bring forth the blessed fruits of the Spirit, to your praise and glory, through Jesus Christ our Lord. Amen.

HENRY ALFORD (1810–71)

O Lord, give me strength to refrain from the unkind silence that is born of hardness of heart; the unkind silence that clouds the serenity of understanding and is the enemy of peace.

Give me the strength to be the first to tender the healing word and the renewal of friendship, that the bonds of amity and the flow of charity may be strengthened . . .

CECIL HUNT

O God our Father, good beyond all that is good, fair beyond all that is fair, in whom is calmness and peace; do thou make up the dissensions which divide us from each other, and bring us back into an unity of love, which may bear some likeness to thy sublime nature.

JACOBITE LITURGY OF ST DIONYSIUS

*Loving Saviour, you taught us that all
things are possible to our heavenly Father.
Strengthen our belief in your words,
especially in the difficult days of our
marriage when fears, mistrust and doubts
arise.*

*Renew our spirits with fresh awakenings of
love, joy, trust and forgiveness.*

*Increase our faith in the power of the Holy
Spirit to make all things new, that by his
grace our marriage may be restored to its
former joy, and together we may give you
thanks and praise.*

MOTHERS' UNION PRAYER BOOK

Lord, we are sorry and we ask your
forgiveness
That sometimes we show lack of respect,
or understanding, or love;
That we neglect each other by neglecting to
pray for each other;
That we have often spoiled the perfect
relationship you planned for us;
And yet we also want to thank you
For the happiness we have known together
For the sadness we have faced together
For the problems we are overcoming
together
For the love which you give us which is
completely unspoiled.
In the name of Jesus Christ, our Lord.

CHRISTOPHER IDLE

Our Relationship
With Others

Dear friends, let us love one another, for love comes from God. Everyone who loves has been born of God and knows God.

FROM THE FIRST LETTER OF JOHN

Almighty and most merciful God, who has given us a new commandment that we should love one another, give us also grace to fulfil it. Make us gentle, courteous and forbearing. Direct our lives so that we may look to the good of others in word and deed. Hallow all our friendships by the blessing of thy Spirit, for the sake of your Son Jesus Christ our Lord.

BISHOP WESTCOTT (1825–1901)

*Dear Lord, who hast blessed us with the
gift of family life that we may learn to love
and care for others: we praise thee for the
example of thy Son Jesus Christ, who even
when deserted and betrayed by closest
friends took thought for his mother and his
disciple. Open our eyes to recognize in all
men the claims of kinship, and stir our
hearts to serve them as brethren called with
us into the sonship of thy love.*

BASIL NAYLOR

*Make us ever eager, Lord, to share the good
things that we have. Grant us such a
measure of your Spirit that we may find
more joy in giving than in getting. Make us
ready to give cheerfully without grudging,
secretly without praise, and in sincerity
without looking to gratitude, for Jesus
Christ's sake.*

JOHN HUNTER (1849–1917)

Be pleased, O Lord, to remember our friends: all that have prayed for us and that have done us good. Do good to them, and return all their kindness double in their own bosom, rewarding them with blessings, sanctifying them with your graces, and bringing them to glory; through Jesus Christ our Lord.

JEREMY TAYLOR (1613–67)

Our Home

The Lord . . . blesses the home of the
righteous.

FROM THE BOOK OF PROVERBS

Peace be to your house,
and to all who shall dwell in it.

Peace be to those who enter,
and to those who go out therefrom.

Peace be to all who love the Lord Jesus
in sincerity.

O God, whose Word compares marriage to the perfect union between Jesus your Son and the church his bride; be present we pray with all those newly married, as they set up a new home together;

Grant them lasting faithfulness to you and to each other; true unity with you and with each other; increasing love for you and for each other;

That they may know that unless the Lord builds the house, the builders' work is all in vain;

And that you will make their homes places where others may meet with yourself; through Jesus Christ our Lord.

CHRISTOPHER IDLE

Almighty Father, we humbly pray for your blessing upon this home. Accept our offering of thanksgiving for the promise of security and happiness which it represents, and fortify our resolve to make it, now and always, a temple dedicated to you. Let it be filled with the beauty of holiness and the warmth of love. May the guest and stranger find within it welcome and friendship. So may it ever merit the praise: 'How lovely are your tents, O Jacob, your dwelling places, O Israel!'

SERVICE OF THE HEART

Heavenly Father, whose Son made his home
among us here on earth: help us to
recognize his presence in this home of ours
which we now dedicate to your service.
Let love abound within its walls.
Grant that in every activity we may have
the seal of your approval.
May all who visit us here find a haven of
joy and peace; and may this our home be a
foretaste of the eternal home which our
Lord Jesus has gone to prepare for us, where
we shall be with him for evermore.

MARTIN PARSONS

Let us thank God:
for the divine institution of family life with
its mutual love and caring, its joy and
support in trouble;
that our Lord Jesus Christ shared the life of
an earthly home, was obedient to Mary and
Joseph, was ready to leave his home at
God's call, and when dying on the cross
made provision for his mother;
for all that Christ and his church mean to
us in our family life;
for the witness to others of the Christian
home.

GEORGE APPLETON

*O God, make the door of this house wide
enough to receive all who need human love
and fellowship; narrow enough to shut out
all envy, pride and strife. Make its
threshold smooth enough to be no
stumbling-block to children, nor to
straying feet, but rugged and strong
enough to turn back the tempter's power.
God make the door of this house the
gateway to thine eternal kingdom.*

ON RUINED ST STEPHEN'S WALBROOK, LONDON

*O God, who art everywhere present, bless
this our home, and help us to remember
that Jesus is always our unseen guest, and
so help us never in this place to do or to say
anything which would make him sad to see.*

WILLIAM BARCLAY

Our Journey
Through Life

Many waters cannot quench love;
rivers cannot wash it away.

FROM THE SONG OF SONGS

O Lord, make your presence felt among us.
Give us courage to live in accordance with
your will, even when shadows fall upon us.
When our own weaknesses and the storms of
life hide you from our sight, take us by the
hand, and teach us that you are near to
each one of us at all times, and especially
when we strive to live truer, gentler and
nobler lives. Give us trust, O Lord; give us
peace, and give us light. May our hearts
find their rest in you.

SERVICE OF THE HEART

Grant unto us, Almighty God, of your good Spirit, that quiet heart, and that patient lowliness to which your comforting Spirit comes; that we, being humble toward you, and loving toward one another, may have our hearts prepared for that peace of yours which passes all understanding; which, if we have, the storms of life can hurt us but little, and the cares of life vex us not at all; in presence of which death shall lose its sting, and the grave its terror; and we, in calm joy, walk all the days of our appointed time, until our great change shall come. Amen.

GEORGE DAWSON (1821–76)

Almighty and most merciful Father, in whom we live and move and have our being, to whose tender compassion we owe our safety in days past, together with all the comforts of the present life, and the hopes of that which is to come . . . Grant, we beseech thee, that Jesus our Lord, the hope of glory, may be formed in us in all humility, meekness, patience, contentedness, and absolute surrender of our souls and bodies to thy holy will and pleasure. Leave us not, nor forsake us, O Father, but conduct us safe through all changes of our condition here, in unchangeable love to thee, and in holy tranquillity of mind in thy love to us, till we come to dwell with thee, and rejoice in thee for ever. Amen.

SIMON PATRICK (1626–1707)

Rest upon us, O Spirit of love, and chase all anger, envy, and bitter grudges from our souls. Be our comforter in trial, when the billows go over our heads; be our strength in the hour of weakness . . . Show us the path wherein we should tread, for if we trust to our own impulses we shall go astray; but if you lead us we shall run in the way of your commandments.

J.F. STARK (1680–1756)

O God, by whom the meek are guided in judgement and light rises up in darkness for the godly; grant us, in all our doubts and uncertainties, the grace to ask what you would have us do; that the Spirit of Wisdom may save us from all false choices and that in your light we may see light and in your straight path may not stumble; through Jesus Christ our Lord.

WILLIAM BRIGHT (1824–1901)

*God of all grace, you gladden our hearts with
the yearly celebration of our wedding day.
Thank you for the mercies of the past.
Help us to treasure the precious memories of
your goodness and faithfulness over the years,
and deepen our love for one another and our
confidence in you. We ask it in the name of
him who brought joy to the wedding feast at
Cana, Jesus Christ our Lord.*

MARTIN PARSONS

For Reflection

I may speak in tongues of men or of angels, but if I am without love, I am a sounding gong or a clanging cymbal. I may have the gift of prophecy and know every hidden truth; I may have faith strong enough to move mountains; but if I have no love, I am nothing. I may dole out all I possess, or even give my body to be burnt, but if I have no love, I am none the better.

Love is patient; love is kind and envies no one. Love is never boastful, nor conceited, nor rude; never selfish, not quick to take offence. Love keeps no score of wrongs; does not gloat over other men's sins, but delights in the truth. There is nothing love cannot face; there is no limit to its faith, its hope, and its endurance.

There are three things that last for ever: faith, hope and love; but the greatest of them all is love.

FROM THE FIRST LETTER TO THE CORINTHIANS

Blessings

The Lord bless you and keep you; the Lord make his face shine upon you and be gracious to you; the Lord turn his face towards you and give you peace.

FROM THE BOOK OF NUMBERS

The Lord sanctify you and bless you, the Lord pour the riches of his grace upon you, that you may please him and live together in holy love to your lives' end. So be it.

JOHN KNOX (1505–72)

The mighty God of Jacob be with you to supplant his enemies, and give you the favour of Joseph. The wisdom and the spirit of Stephen be with your heart and with your mouth, and teach your lips what they shall say, and how to answer all things. He is our God, if we despair in ourselves and trust in him; and his is the glory.

WILLIAM TYNDALE (C.1492–1536)

Hear our prayer, O Lord:
bless, protect and sanctify
all those who bow their heads before you.
Through the grace, mercy and love
of your only-begotten Son,
to whom with you and your most holy,
gracious and life-giving Spirit
be blessing now and for ever,
to the ages of ages. Amen.

EASTERN ORTHODOX CHURCH